Little Stories for Little Children

Little Stories for Little Children

A Worship Resource

Donna McKee Rhodes

HERALD PRESS
Scottdale, Pennsylvania
Waterloo, Ontario

Library of Congress Cataloging-in-Publication Data
Rhodes, Donna McKee, 1962-
    Little stories for little children : a worship resource / Donna
McKee Rhodes.
        p.   cm.
        ISBN 0-8361-9000-9 (alk. paper)
        1. Children's sermons. 2. Storytelling in Christian
    education
I. Title.
BV4315.R46 1995
252'.53—dc20   94-38280

The paper used in this publication is recycled and meets the minimum
requirements of American National Standard for Information Sciences—
Permanence of Paper for Printed Library Materials, ANSI Z39.48-1984.

LITTLE STORIES FOR LITTLE CHILDREN
Copyright © 1995 by Herald Press, Scottdale, Pa. 15683
    Published simultaneously in Canada by Herald Press,
    Waterloo, Ont. N2L 6H7. All rights reserved
Library of Congress Catalog Number: 94-38280
International Standard Book Number: 0-8361-9000-9
Printed in the United States of America
Book and cover design by Paula M. Johnson
05 04 03 02 01 00 00 99   10 9 8 7 6 5 4 3

To order or request information, please call
1-800-759-4447 (individuals); 1-800-245-7894 (trade).
Website: www.mph.org

To my children—
Erica, Aaron, and Joel,
whose joy for life constantly reminds me
that we all can have the same
joy as children of God.

Contents

Preface and Acknowledgments

MY HOPE IS THAT THIS collection of stories will aid you in your children's ministry, whether it be in a worship time, church school classroom, or a family home. Use the stories as they are or as a springboard for an idea of your own. Blessings to you as you minister with children!

These stories were written to match with a Scripture or theme of a morning worship service at Stone Church of the Brethren. The two pastors I worked with while developing the stories were Dawn Ottoni Wilhelm and Earle W. Fike, Jr. I appreciate working with Dawn and Earle on the staff at Stone Church, as well as with Judy Cooper, the administrative secretary. The support they provide as fellow staff members is special.

My heartfelt thanks to my husband, Loren, for all of his encouragement in this project and for his computer knowledge, which was greatly helpful in compiling these stories into a collection.

—*Donna Mckee Rhodes*
Huntingdon, Pennsylvania

Introduction

WHAT A PRIVILEGE we have as pastors, Christian educators, and parents to teach and model God's great love to children. It is a pleasure for me to sit on the steps in the sanctuary of Stone Church of the Brethren and watch the children gather around for the story during a Sunday morning worship. A story during worship is an excellent tool to teach God's love and biblical truths to children. During a story time the children also feel the love and acceptance of their church family.

I believe a children's story should be concise, easy to follow, and contain only one main point. Such qualities enable everyone—both children and the adults—to remain focused on the theme. This also allows the storyteller to retain control of the story time. A storyteller must be prepared for any action or any response when young children are involved!

I believe that interaction such as having the children answer questions is valuable in a story time. But structure and a limited amount of response is helpful in keeping the attention of all the children.

I also value active learning in stories when appropriate. For instance, inviting the children to share in the completion of a food item (The Creation Mix), blowing bubbles, (The Breath of God), and selecting a "treasure" from a box (Hidden Treasures) encourages children to be actively involved in the story within a structured setting.

Active learning can have a valuable part in story-telling and instruction for scriptural reasons. Jesus taught by active learning in the feeding of the five thousand and the foot washing.

On occasion, I give a treat to the children such as M & M's (It's Good to Share), or stickers (After Christmas). Always be sure to plan extra treats in case you have visitors!

A picture file is a wonderful resource to develop for use during children's stories. Church school picture pages, magazines, and bulletin covers provide a wealth of possible illustrations for the stories.

My stories most often end with a prayer that emphasizes and restates the theme of the story. I almost always begin the prayer with, "Dear God." I believe that through our storytelling we teach children to have a personal relationship with God which is developed by prayer. Beginning the prayers with a common form of address such as "Dear" emphasizes that God is easily reached by all of us, even children.

Some stories include details from the way they were originally told as a way of showing how local contexts can enrich the stories. However, the stories are intended to be useful in a broad variety of settings. When helpful they are accompanied by instructions for shaping them to fit particular uses.

The stories do not rigidly follow the church year.

But storytellers looking for material for Easter, Mother's Day, Thanksgiving, Advent, or Christmas will find them at roughly the places one would expect if treating the fifty-two stories as representing fifty-two weeks.

Little
Stories for
Little
Children

1

*E*very Day Is New

Object New calendar
Scripture Ephesians 4:22-24
Theme Each Day Is New with God

GOOD MORNING! This week is the start of a new year! Only God knows what exciting new things are in store for us throughout the coming months.

I brought a new calendar with me today. This calendar doesn't have anything written on it yet. Soon there will be notes about meetings, and games, and other things my family will have planned to do.

But right now it is clean with no marks on it at all. Each day of the new year, all 365 days, have the chance to be wonderful days.

At the beginning of the new year, many people make resolutions. The word *resolution* means to promise to try to do something better.

Some people promise to eat better. Some people promise not to yell at other people. Some people promise to read the Bible more.

Even though we really mean well when we make these resolutions or promises, sometimes we break the promise. We quit doing what we said we were going to do better.

But, the wonderful thing about God is that each day is a new beginning. We don't have to start new just on New Year's day. Everyday is a chance to start new with God.

When we make mistakes, God forgives us. God always loves us and never takes that love away. If we don't do well on one day, we can try to do better the next day.

God is wonderfully loving and forgiving. With 365 days in this new year, we have 365 chances to start new with God.

Let's pray—

Dear God, our new year is exciting. Thank you that everyday is a new day with you. Guide us in this new year. Amen.

2

Creation Recipe

Object Large bowl, spoon, Kix cereal, miniature
    marshmallows, chocolate chips, coconut, M & M's,
    fish crackers, animal crackers, raisins

Scripture Genesis 1

Theme God's Creation of the World

*D*O ANY OF YOU LIKE TO HELP your moms
and dads in the kitchen?

It's fun to cook together. As you cook, you follow a
recipe to create something. You might create a cake,
cookies, or another kind of good food. Do you taste
your food and say "MMMM—this is really good!"?

The first story in the Bible tells us of God's creation
of the heavens and earth. On six days of the week God
was busy creating. God didn't follow a recipe, but God
did have a plan.

To help us remember God's plan of creation, let's
make this creation recipe.

*(Invite each child to have a turn in adding an ingredient
or stirring the mixture.)*

On the first day God said, "Let there be light."
When the light was created God saw it was good.

Let's put the Kix cereal in the bowl. The Kix are yellow to represent light.

On the second day God said, "Let there be an expanse to separate water from water." And so God created the sky and saw it was good.

Let's put the marshmallows in the mix to represent the clouds in the sky.

On the third day God said, "Let there be dry ground." When the ground was created, God saw it was good.

Let's put the chocolate chips in the mix to represent the hills and rocks of land.

Then God decided the land needed to produce plants.

Let's put the green tinted coconut in the mix to represent grass.

On the fourth day God said, "Let there be lights in the sky." The sun, moon, and stars were created and God saw it was good.

Let's put the M & M's in the mix to represent the sun, moon, and stars.

On the fifth day God said, "Let the water be filled with living creatures." The fish of the sea and the birds of the air were created and God saw it was good.

Let's put the fish crackers in the mix to represent this day of creation.

On the sixth day God said, "Let the land produce living creatures according to their kinds." All of the animals were created and God saw it was good.

Let's put the animal crackers in the mix to represent the animals of the world.

Then God said, "Let us make man in our image to rule over all the creatures." God created humans and saw it was very good.

Let's put the raisins in the mixture to represent humans.

God's creation was complete and on the seventh day God rested. God's creation is magnificent and very beautiful for us.

We have a creation in our bowl to help us remember God's wonderful creation. After the worship service, each of you come back to me and I will give you some of our creation mix.

Let's pray—

Dear God, your creation is wonderful and we thank you for it. Amen.

3 *BRC 9-22-23*
*B*reath of God

Object   A bottle of bubbles
Scripture   Genesis 2:7
Theme   God's Breath Is in Each of Us

*D*O YOU LIKE TO BLOW BUBBLES? *(Blow a few bubbles. Let the children enjoy the bubbles floating.)*

Bubbles are fun. I think everyone likes bubbles. It is not hard to smile when you see someone blowing bubbles and watch the bubbles float through the air.

There are a couple of ways to blow bubbles. One is to blow gently and watch the bubbles float away from the wand. Another way is to blow a bubble with bubble gum. Have you ever had a drinking straw in a cup? You can blow your breath through the straw and watch bubbles come up from the drink.

All of those ways to make bubbles have one thing in common. That is they all were blown with breath. All of those bubbles are created by someone blowing breath into them.

The Bible story we are hearing today tells of God forming a person from dust and breathing into the person to create a living being. God gave the person the breath of life.

We all have a little bit of God's breath inside us.

God didn't give breath to us like he did the first human being, but God did give us life and that is part of God's breath.

God doesn't really breathe like we do. But talking about God's breath is a way to talk about God wanting to give us life and his desire for us to keep growing. When we learn Bible stories, listen in church school and our worship service, and pray and think about God, we are keeping the breath of God alive in us. Not only are you growing physically, but you can grow spiritually as well when you think and learn about God.

Let's pray—

Dear God, thank you for the breath of life. Help us to keep growing. Amen.

4

*T*hings Change

Object Kaleidoscope
Scripture Exodus 14:5-15
Theme Don't Resist Change

*T*HIS STORY WAS TOLD as a pastoral change was about to take place. If the group is small enough, pass the kaleidoscope around for all the children to see.

How many of you have ever looked through a kaleidoscope? What do you see when you look in it? *(Wait for children's responses.)*

You see a pretty pattern. As you move it the pattern changes. The old pattern was very nice, but the new pattern is nice, too. The colors move easily into a new pattern. They don't resist changing into a new shape of design.

Just as the colors change into a new design, we have changes in our lives that we need to deal with. You might experience change at school when you move to a new classroom or get a new teacher. You experience change as you grow. You wouldn't want to stay little forever. It is fun to think about growing up. Adults have changes in their lives, too.

There are a couple of ways to deal with change.

One is to want things to stay the way they have always been and not want change to happen. Another way is to think about how things have been—but decide it is okay to try something new. We can look forward rather than backward.

God has a big plan for each of us. We can remember that God is working out that plan as our lives change.

When you are facing a change in your life, try to move into that change as easily as the colors move into a new pattern in a kaleidoscope. God is working out a special plan for you.

Let's pray—

Dear God, we know you are working in each of our lives. Help us adjust to the changes you have planned for us. Amen.

5

God Wants to Be Number One

Object Holiday/toy catalog
Scripture Exodus 20:3
Theme Put God First in Your Life

D O ANY OF YOU GET EXCITED when a toy catalog comes to your house? It's exciting to look at the fun and special toys, isn't it?

It's okay to have that excitement, but sometimes it's easy for us to decide we want something and that we absolutely have to have it. We think if we don't get it, our lives will be awful.

When we want something very badly, it's easy to let that thing be the most important thing in our lives. Sometimes people let their favorite possession or dream be number one in their lives. Some grown-ups may want to have a special car or fancy clothes or certain furniture. Some children may really want a special bike, a beautiful doll, or a great video game.

Even though those special things seem really important, we should remember always to let God be number one in our lives. God wants to be number one in our lives. God wants to be more important to you than your favorite toy or your favorite clothes or your favorite television show.

There is a commandment in the Bible that says "You shall have no other gods before me."

Sometimes the favorite possession or dream that we talked about earlier becomes so important to somebody that it seems like a god. And then people sometimes forget to worship the real God.

When we put God first in our lives, we are remembering to live the way he wants us to live. God wants us to love him more than things. When we love God more than things, God leads us to peace and happiness.

Let's pray—

Dear God, it is easy to love things. Help us to love you more. Amen.

6
*G*od *Talks to Us*

Object Portable phone
Scripture 1 Samuel 3:1-20
Theme God Is Always Willing to Talk to Us

DO YOU KNOW WHAT THIS IS? It is a phone. There are many different types of phones. This is a portable phone that lets you move around when you are talking. With some phones you need to stay where the phone is connected to the jack.

Some of you know how to use a phone and others are learning. When the phone rings at your house, it is a mystery who is calling. It is fun to answer to discover who is calling.

Have you ever heard a grown-up say, "God called me to do something"? Do you think God used a phone to do that?

Sometimes people feel called by God to do work for the church. That doesn't mean God called them on their phone. But people do sometimes feel God is talking to them. Or they feel God is guiding them to do the work.

Not only can God talk to us or guide us, but we are also given the gift of being able to talk to God.

And you don't need to be a grown-up to talk to

God. God wants to hear from each of you, too. We can talk to God as much as we like. It doesn't need to be a special time of the day. It can be anytime or anywhere.

We don't need a special phone, or phone number. And our connection to God is never busy. God is always willing to listen to us when we talk to him through prayer.

Let's pray—

Dear God, what a great thing it is to be able to talk to you anytime. Thank you for always listening. Amen.

7 *Children Have Power*

Object List of good/bad word phrases
Scripture Psalm 19:14
Theme Children Can Choose Between Good Power and Bad Power

*L*ET'S START WITH A QUESTION. What is the most powerful thing you know of? *(The children's answers will often have to do with physical strength as a form of power—tackling, running, etc.)*

Do you know that even children have a lot of power? You have physical power to run, throw a ball, and do other physical activities.

You use brain power when you read, think, and do other schoolwork and activities.

We also have word power, which can be either good or bad.

Let's try something—I'm going to tell you some words and you say if these words are using good or bad word power. Are you ready?

That's really stupid! *(Wait for children's response and praise them for correct answer.)*

It was really kind of you to help me.

That kid can't throw a ball at all!

You made a really nice picture.

All of you did a good job knowing about good and bad word power!

The words we use have effect or power on other people. Have any of you had a time when someone said mean things to you or they got angry with you? Did they show their anger to you?

How did you feel? You probably felt sad and maybe angry, too. Mean and unkind words have power to make people sad or angry.

But just think what power good words can have on people! When you use kind words to tell someone they have been nice to you or that they look nice, you make them feel happy.

Would you rather use mean word power or good word power? I think we all prefer good word power.

Try each day to use good word power on someone. You will make them feel happy and you will feel happy, too.

Let's pray—

Dear God, please show us ways to use good word power and help us forget bad word power. Amen.

8

Shelter Under Wings

Object Picture of a white-browed sparrow weaver
found in a bird identification book

Scripture Psalm 57:1

Theme God Provides Care

*T*HIS STORY WAS USED DURING a morning
worship which included a child/parent dedication.

Look at this picture with me. It is a picture of a bird
in Africa called a white-browed sparrow weaver.

The parent birds care very deeply for their young.
They live in Africa where it is difficult to find food to
survive. Finding food requires much work on the part
of the parents. There are times when the babies must
be left alone for most of a day while parents search for
food.

To be sure their babies are cared for while they are
gone, the parents have a unique way of building a nest.
The nest is always built on the western side of the tree.

This is great for the birds. The parents can keep
them warm when the sun is not up. But while the parents are gone, the rays from the sun keep the nest
warm. The birds instinctively know to build the nest in
this way.

God provides care for the babies from the warmth of the sun. In the lives of these white-browed sparrow weavers, the birds don't provide all the care for the babies. God helps provide care through the warm sun.

It is the same way with humans. Parents provide much of the care for children, but they trust God to help them. God provides the parents with wisdom, guidance, and ability to raise children. God also provides a church family where children can be raised.

All of us in this church family care a lot for all of you. You are all part of our church family. All of your life, God will continue to guide the church family, your parents—and you.

Remember that God is always present in your lives, guiding, helping, and protecting.

Let's pray—

Dear God, thank you for parents who love us, a church family who cares about us, and your constant guidance and protection. Amen.

9
God's Helping Hands

Object A circle of hand shapes from church members (should be constructed before the story)

Scripture Psalm 90:17

Theme Every Hand Can Do Work for God

I HAVE WITH ME A CIRCLE OF HANDS. These hands are from a variety of people. Our pastor's hand is on this circle. My hand, the organist's hand, and the church secretary's hand are on here also. Yesterday when the church board was together, everyone outlined their hand to be included on this circle. And this morning some of you outlined your hand in church school.

There are a lot of hands on this circle. It would have been nice to try to get a hand outline from everyone in our church. Each one of us has wonderful talents that help to serve God. Our hands are very important in using our talents. All of these hands do important work for God.

Some hands help to plan for our church. Some hands teach. All of the hands reach out to help other people. There are all sizes of hands on this circle. Some are large and some are small. But all of these hands do work for God.

All in this congregation could have put their hands on this circle because we all, even little children, can do work for God. All of us can use our talents and our hands to worship and serve God. Our hands are the only hands God has to get his work done on earth.

Let's pray—
Dear God, thank you for our hands that do so many things. Help us use our hands for your work. Amen.

10 *We Need to Watch Our Guidelines*

Object   A picture of lines painted on a road
Scripture   Psalm 119:33-40
Theme   The Bible Gives Us Guidelines

ONE DAY THIS WEEK AS I WAS DRIVING, I was thinking about how important it is to follow the rules to drive safely. The road is painted with lines. This picture is one example of lines on a road.

Do you know what the white lines along the edge of the road mean? What about the yellow lines in the middle of the road?

These lines are painted on the road to give the drivers guidelines. If a driver crosses too far over the white lines along the edge of the road, he or she may hit something. And, if the driver crosses over the middle yellow line, he or she may hit another car.

If the yellow line is in dashes, it means it is okay to cross into the other lane to pass another car because there is no traffic in that lane.

All of the lines provide guidelines for drivers.

You are small to remember all these rules about driving. But just as the lines on the road provide guidelines for the drivers, there are guidelines for us to follow in our lives.

We all know we need to try to live a Christian life. The Bible provides us with guidelines to live that life. We learn these guidelines in church school, during morning worship, and from our parents.

It is not always easy to follow these guidelines. When we cross over the lines set by the Bible, we get in trouble, just like the drivers who cross over the lines on the road.

One thing that makes it easier for us to follow guidelines is God's constant presence in our lives. With God's help and guidance, we will follow the right guidelines.

Let's pray—

Dear God, please keep us in the guidelines of life. Amen.

11

Twenty-Four Hour Care

Object   Teddy bear
Scripture   Psalm 121:3-4
Theme   God Constantly Watches Over Us

I BROUGHT A TEDDY BEAR with me today. This teddy bear is special to someone in our family. Most all children have a special teddy bear, doll, or blanket.

Do each of you have something that is special to you? Do you keep your special bear or doll or blanket in bed with you at night?

You know your special item will stay with you at night. It will be with you when you wake up and it can go with you wherever you want to take it.

The bear gives you some security. Some children have special blankets that they keep with them to feel safe. Sometimes those blankets are called security blankets.

There is another kind of security we have which we can't see. This security stays with us all the time. We can take it along with us wherever we go.

This security is God. There is a verse in the Bible that says God doesn't sleep. God doesn't even take a nap. That means God is awake all the time and constantly watches over us. God never goes on vacation and never takes a coffee break. God is always watching over us.

It is fine to have a teddy bear or a blanket as security. And knowing God is never sleeping and always watching over us gives us extra special security.

Let's pray—

Dear God, thank you for caring so much for us that you constantly watch over us. Amen.

12

Do Your Best

Object Pencil, eraser, paper
Scripture Ecclesiastes 9:10
Theme Do the Best You Can Do in Everything

I REALLY LIKE ERASERS. This is my special eraser that I use a lot. It is very helpful to me. Whenever I write something and realize I have made a mistake, I can use my eraser and take my mistake away. *(Demonstrate by writing something and then erasing it.)*

Just because I have an eraser doesn't mean I should be careless and not do a good job. I always try to do my best and write correctly. But when I make a mistake, I can use my eraser.

There are two ways we can do something. We can do our best or we can do less than our best. Which does God want? You are right! God wants us to do the best we can.

In the Bible, in Ecclesiastes 9:10, it says, "Whatever your hand finds to do, do it with all your might." God wants the best in everything we do. At home, school, church, or play, always do your best. That is the only way you will be satisfied with the things you do. It pleases God when we give him our best. Let's do our best to please God.

But often we make mistakes even when we are trying our best to please God. Then, just like my eraser, God helps us. When we tell God we are sorry about a mistake, God forgives us just like the eraser took away the mistake.

We know that God is forgiving and loves us even when we make a mistake. With God's guidance we can try our best to do our best.

Let's pray—

Dear God, guide us to do our best and help us through our mistakes. Amen.

13
*W*isdom from Older Folks

Object Picture of grandparent and grandchild
Scripture Ecclesiastes 12:1-7
Theme Older People Are Special People

I HAVE A PICTURE WITH ME TODAY. Can you read the words on the picture? *(Adjust the opening paragraph according to your picture.)*

In this picture, a grandfather and his grandson are sitting together on a step. It looks like they are having a special conversation.

Each of you probably have grandmothers and grandfathers with whom you have a good time when you visit with each other. Sometimes we may have other special friends who are older people. I have heard them called grandfriends.

We can learn many things from our grandparents or grandfriends. They have had a lot of experience in life and can share a lot of wisdom with us. Grandparents have done many things in their lives and have seen many changes that they can tell us about.

Grandparents usually have many stories to tell about when they were young. A lot of things that we take for granted today did not exist when grandparents were young. They didn't have a microwave or a

VCR. They didn't have fancy toys like are available today.

But grandparents do have many special stories, ideas, and especially a lot of love to share with you.

Enjoy time you might spend with grandparents or grandfriends. Not only can you learn from them, but they like being around you and hearing about your life, too.

Let's pray—

Dear God, thank you for grandparents and grandfriends who love and care for us. Amen.

14

*W*e *Still Have Excitement*

Object   Palm branch for each child
Scripture   Matthew 21: 1-11
Theme   Jesus Still Lives with Us Today

This could begin in either of two ways:

1. The children could be given palm branches and be in a procession as the service begins. Begin the story by talking about the procession carrying palm branches and compare to the palm Sunday procession in the Bible.

2. Distribute the palm branches as the children gather for the story. Give the children opportunity to wave the branches at the beginning of the story.

Adjust the first paragraph according to which beginning you choose.

YOU DID SOMETHING SPECIAL this morning when you came in with the palms. What was it like to carry the palms? Was it fun? Was it exciting?

During the Scripture reading, we heard the Bible story of Jesus coming to the city of Jerusalem. He wanted to tell the people about God. Jesus was able to tell all about God's love. Many of the people in Jerusalem had already heard about Jesus. They knew of the good things he had done. They were excited when Jesus came to Jerusalem.

When Jesus came, the people wanted to do or say something because they couldn't keep their excitement inside them. So the people ran to greet Jesus and shouted, "Hosanna! Blessings on him who comes in the name of the Lord!"

Hosanna means "save us" or "keep us safe." Many thought Jesus was a new leader who would protect them from their enemies. They treated him like a king.

As Jesus rode by on his donkey, some people took their coats off and laid them on the ground for him to ride over. Others tore branches from palm trees and waved them in the air, shouting "Hosanna."

Today we still think of Jesus as a king. In fact, we call him the "King of Kings." The people in Jerusalem long ago were excited because Jesus was with them. We know that Jesus is still with us today and that is something to be excited about!

Let's pray—

Dear God, let us always be excited because of Jesus. Amen.

15

*S*hare a Great Gift

Object A small, foil-wrapped candy egg for each child

Scripture Mark 16

Theme Easter Is a Time of Sharing

GOOD MORNING AND HAPPY EASTER! Did each of you get some candy in a basket this morning?

Let me tell you a story about candy eggs. Sometime ago, a town held an Easter egg hunt for its children. The children were told that among the eggs hidden, were twelve gold, foil-wrapped Easter eggs. Whoever found any of these eggs would receive a special prize.

Of course, all of the children searched with all their might. Everyone found plain eggs, and a few children found the gold eggs.

There were two little boys who saw a gold egg at the same time. Both boys knew the other had seen the egg. This created a problem because they both wanted that egg.

They looked at each other and at the egg. Finally the boy who was just a little bit older reached for the egg and put it in the younger boy's basket. The youngest boy was happy and ran off to get his special prize.

The older boy was a little sad that he couldn't keep the egg for himself. But he knew he had made someone else very happy and that felt good. He knew he had shared something special.

Today is Easter and a time to remember how special it was for Jesus to share his life with us. Jesus went to the cross, and died for his people with a lot of pain.

But Jesus also rose again to share his life and promise of eternal life for us. What a great job of sharing that was!

Let's pray—

Dear God, we thank you for the special message of Easter and the sharing that Jesus did for us. Amen.

16

K *eep Your Temper Under Control*

Object Thermometer
Scripture Habakkuk 1:1-3
Theme Control Your Temper

DO YOU KNOW WHAT THIS IS? It is a thermometer. There are many kinds of thermometers.

This is a thermometer that measures the temperature of the air. As the air gets warmer, the red part of the thermometer, or the mercury, increases.

Then there is the kind to take your temperature with when you are sick. And in our refrigerator, we have a thermometer shaped like a milk carton to measure the coldness of the refrigerator.

But you know, there is not a thermometer to measure our hot tempers.

Do you know what a temper is? A rising temper is when you feel angry at someone or something and you just want to yell or do something else to let all of your anger out of your body.

Maybe your mother or father sometimes says to you, "Watch your temper!" or "Don't throw a temper tantrum!" Probably every parent has said those words at some point.

A temper can sometimes get the best of us. Then we might say or do things that we will later feel badly about.

It is okay to let persons know we are angry with them by telling them but not letting our temper get the best of us. It isn't good to keep angry feelings locked up inside of us so we should tell other people when something irritates us.

But we can get rid of our angry feelings without a flare-up in our temper. When we become angry we need to work at forgiving the person we are angry with.

Sometimes temper can lead to violence. Then someone's body or feelings may be hurt. When that happens, a lot of people feel badly.

That's not what God wants to happen. God wants us to control our tempers and live peacefully together. With God's help we all can keep our tempers in check.

Let's pray—
Dear God, we do want to live peacefully. Help us keep our tempers in check. Amen.

17

Giving Makes Everyone Happy

Object A marshmallow for each child
Scripture John 10:18
Theme Find Ways to Give Joy

TO START OUR TIME TOGETHER, I am going to give each of you a marshmallow. It is okay to eat it now, or you can save it if you want to. *(Pass out the marshmallows.)*

How did you feel when I gave you the marshmallow? *(Expect smiles and responses such as happy, surprised, and excited.)* It is good to give to other people. Giving to other people makes them happy, and you feel happy, too.

There are many ways we can give to other people and make them happy. When we help them, we are giving our time. Sometimes, we actually give something that they can hold in their hands. There are other times when we give something they can't hold such as a smile, a hug or kiss. By giving to other people, whether it can be something they can hold in their hands or something they can't hold, you are giving them a gift and you are sharing God's love. The person you gave something to is happy because you shared with them. You feel happy because you gave a gift. And, God is happy, too, because you have given and shared his love.

Today, find a way to give something to another person. Maybe what you give will be a smile, maybe a hug, maybe a song, or maybe it will be a picture you drew. Find a way to give and remember, when you kindly give something to another person you are also giving God's love.

Let's pray—

Dear God, thank you for all you have given to us. Help us to find ways to give to other people. Amen.

18

*B*e Like a Dandelion

Object Dandelions or a picture of dandelions
Scripture Matthew 5:13-16
Theme Christians Can "Pop Up" Like Dandelions

W E ARE BEGINNING TO SEE many signs of springtime. Spring is a very beautiful time of year. The trees are growing leaves. Some flowers are blooming. And the grass is getting green.

In our front yard, the grass is a nice shade of green, but there are little yellow flowers popping up all over our front lawn. Do you know what kind of flower I'm talking about? *(dandelion)*

Have you ever picked a bouquet of dandelions for your mom? This time of year, it seems as though dandelions are all over the place.

Some people try to get rid of the dandelions in their yard. They dig out and try to kill the root.

But you know what? Those dandelions are really stubborn. They not only want to stay where they are growing, but they like to grow other places too.

Dandelions aren't cared for like we care for other flowers, but they keep growing. They will grow just about anywhere. We see those little yellow happy flowers all over the place.

Maybe we as Christians should be more like dandelions. We can pop up like dandelions in places where we can be helpful and true like Jesus was.

When you are honest, or helpful, or kind, you are a Christian popping up like a dandelion. Try to find a place to be a dandelion today.

Let's pray—

Dear God, there are many places where we can show by our actions that we believe in you. Guide us, God, and show us where we can be dandelions. Amen.

19

The Same, Yet Changed

Object A Toy That Changes Form
Scripture Matthew 17:1-13
Theme Things Are Not Always as They Appear

TODAY I BROUGHT A TOY that belongs to my son. What would you call this toy? Would you say it looks like a truck?

That's what it looks like to me. But if I push this button, the van transforms into a helicopter.

We must be careful with this kind of toy and look closely before we decide what it is. Because what it is when we first see it may change when we look again.

Today, during the Scripture reading, you heard the word "transfiguration." That is a really big word. But it has to do simply with something that has been changed from one thing to another.

The Bible tells us that Jesus was "transfigured." As the disciples watched, Jesus' appearance changed. He looked different from before. His face and clothes were so bright they looked like sunshine.

When you hear the word "transfiguration," think of how the toy changed. Remember that looking again is important because things are not always like we think they are at first. Sometimes things look different when we look at them a second time.

Remember when Jesus was transfigured, he looked different from before. The disciples saw Jesus in a new and wonderful way.

Let's pray—

Dear God, help us remember things are not always as we think they are at first. Help us to see them in other ways. Amen.

20

Caring Like a Shepherd

Object A picture of Jesus with sheep
Scripture Isaiah 40:11
Theme Mothers Guide Us Like Shepherds

I BROUGHT A PICTURE THAT I have had for a long time. I was given this picture as a gift from a Sunday School teacher when I was about three or four years old. *(Adapt the opening paragraph according to your picture of Jesus and sheep.)*

The picture shows Jesus with sheep. And we can see the kind and loving nature of Jesus by the way he is caring for these sheep. See how gently he is carrying the lamb in his arms. All of the other sheep are gathered closely by Jesus' feet.

A shepherd has an important job. The shepherd cares for the sheep by feeding them, not letting them wander too far away, and by caring for them when they've been hurt.

As children, we don't need a shepherd like sheep, but we do need a mother. A mother does some of the same jobs a shepherd does. A mother feeds her children and keeps track of where they are.

A mother gives her children guidance and she protects her children to the best of her ability.

There are many ways a mother shows she loves her children. Not only is a mother's love shown by hugs and kisses and saying "I love you," but it is also shown by all she does for her children.

Today is Mother's Day. This is a day to remember and thank your mother for all she does for you. You can show you love your mother by hugs and kisses and doing nice things for her. And you can say thank you to God for your mother.

Let's pray—

Dear God, thank you for our mothers who guide us and love us like shepherds. Amen.

21

No One Should Be Hungry

Object Picture of the World or a Globe
Scripture Matthew 25:34-35
Theme World Hunger

THIS IS A PICTURE OF THE WORLD. The world is very big and there are many, many people in it. It is hard for children to understand how big the world is.

But one thing that is not hard to understand is that though children throughout the world might have different skin color, they are the same in many ways. One of the ways children all over the world are alike is that they all need food to grow.

All of you are very lucky because you have a lot of food to eat. Some children in the world don't have enough to eat. Because they don't have enough to eat, they don't have much energy to play like you do.

Hunger in the world is a very sad thing. Jesus tells us in the Bible to feed the hungry people.

You may have noticed a box outside the sanctuary door. Our church helps to feed the hungry by giving food to the community food bank. People bring some packaged food and put it in that box. Then a volunteer from church takes all the food to the community food bank. That is a great way to help feed the hungry.

Each of you can help feed the hungry by bringing a can of food for the food bank when you come to church next Sunday. Put it in the big box and it will be taken to the food bank.

(If your church does not have an on-going food collection program, perhaps you could coordinate a one-time collection of canned food for a food bank or other social organization.)

This is one way we can help feed the hungry people. Jesus said to love one another. By helping to feed the hungry, you are showing love.

Let's pray—

Dear God, we thank you that we have enough food to eat. Help us to find ways to help those who are hungry. Amen.

22
*M*anipulation

Object Magnet, paper clip, stiff paper

Scripture Matthew 26:57-68

Theme People Shouldn't Manipulate Others for Their Own Way

*D*O ANY OF YOU KNOW WHAT THIS IS? It is a magnet. I also brought with me a piece of paper and a paper clip. *(Be ready to demonstrate.)*

If I lay this paper clip on the paper, it doesn't move. But if I put the magnet under the paper and move it, the paper clip follows the magnet. The paper clip does what the magnet does.

We can say the magnet manipulates the paper clip. That means the magnet can make the paper clip do something.

Some people manipulate other people with their words or actions. They use their words and actions to get other people to do what they want.

People who manipulate are not living the way Jesus wants them to live. It is not right for us to hurt other people by manipulating them just to get what we want.

We need to remember that other people have feelings. By manipulating people's feelings, we can hurt those people.

Let's all try to live the way Jesus wants us to live and not manipulate someone else just to get our own way.

Let's pray—
Dear God, help us realize that other people's feelings are important and that we should not manipulate people to get our own way. Amen.

23

*H*ave a Good Attitude!

Object Picture of a smiling person
Scripture Mark 10:46-52
Theme A Good Attitude Is Important

*E*VERYBODY GET READY, BECAUSE I am going to ask you to do something. Let's see a great big smile! That's great! I am really happy to see each one of you. I enjoy our special time together on Sunday mornings.

Have any of you had your picture taken recently? Did the photographer ask you to smile? Most people smile when they get their picture taken.

A smile is a good thing. It makes other people feel happy. It is easier to smile than to frown. And a smile shows a good attitude. That means you are in a good mood and feel positive.

We all have times when we feel sad. Sometimes it seems as though there aren't things to smile about.

What we can do then is remember God's constant presence in our lives. We remember that God is always with us. We know God is with us when we are happy, or sad, or feeling sick.

Knowing that God is always with us is something to smile about. We can be grateful for God's blessings and faithfulness even when things don't go our way.

When we keep a good attitude, our life will seem brighter even when we face trouble. We can remember that God is with us all the time. That is definitely something to have a good attitude about!

Let's pray—

Dear God, remind us of the many things in life for which we can smile. Help us to always keep a good attitude. Amen.

24

*R*ecognizing Jesus

Object Pictures of Jesus
Scripture Luke 2:22-40
Theme We See Jesus in Many Ways

Have a variety of pictures of Jesus. Be sure to have pictures in which Jesus is shown in different styles. Some possible resources are church school curriculum, bulletin covers, pictures in children's Bibles, and other artwork.

*A*RTISTS HAVE DRAWN OR PAINTED Jesus in ways they believe Jesus looks. Each of us has an idea in our mind of how Jesus looks. These are pictures in which Jesus is easily recognized. There are other places in life where we can see Jesus.

We can see Jesus in the people around us. We see Jesus when people try to do what is right like being honest and fair and caring.

Sometimes it is hard to see Jesus in the lives of others, especially when they don't act loving. But when we look hard enough, there will be something to remind us of Jesus. Maybe it is a reminder of how we need to be kind.

We come to church to recognize Jesus more easily. The hymns, stories, Bible readings, and prayers during our worship service all help us know Jesus better.

When we think about it, we see Jesus in all kinds of places. When we see loving faces around us, we see Jesus. When someone helps us, we see Jesus. When others are kind, we see Jesus.

Let's pray—

Dear God, there are so many places in our lives where we can recognize Jesus. Help us to see him clearly. Amen.

25

God Gives Us New Energy

Object Flashlight with dead batteries, new batteries for replacement

Scripture Luke 13:7-8

Theme God Recharges Our Soul

*H*AS YOUR FAMILY EVER NEEDED a flashlight when the lights aren't working? Or maybe you have used a flashlight camping.

Let's turn this flashlight on. What happened? I pushed the button, but the light didn't come on. What do you think? I need new batteries? Let's try that. Ah, you were right! The flashlight works fine now!

When batteries don't work, they can be fixed in one of two ways. New batteries can be used in place of the old batteries. Or some batteries can be recharged with a special machine.

People don't run on batteries like toys and some other things do. But sometimes we run down like batteries and feel as though we need to be recharged.

There are many reasons why we feel we need to be recharged. Maybe we are sad, discouraged, or tired. At these times it is easy to feel badly about ourselves.

We can't plug into a recharger like batteries. But we have some place where we can go when we feel like we need to be recharged. God helps us to feel recharged. A worship service with stories, songs, and prayers helps us to feel recharged. We know people in our church family care about us. The care from other people can help recharge us.

Church isn't the only place we can feel recharged. We can talk to God in prayer whenever we want. We can tell God everything that we are feeling. God wants us to talk to him in prayer.

Reading the Bible will also recharge us. The Bible has many wonderful words and thoughts that will give us new energy.

When batteries run down, they need to be attached to a recharger. We are fortunate that God is constantly with us. We can go to God whenever we want to be recharged.

Let's pray—

Dear God, your constant presence in our lives is special to us. Keep us charged like batteries so we may do work for you. Amen.

26
Loving Care

Object Picture of mother hen and chicks

Scripture Luke 13:34

Theme God Gives Us the Same Love as a Mother Hen Gives Her Chicks

I AM SURE EVERYONE KNOWS what kind of animal is in this picture. You're right—chickens. It is a picture of a mother hen and her chicks.

A mother hen gives special care to her chicks. The chicks remain in eggs for three weeks. The mother hen carefully sits on the eggs to keep them safe and warm so the chicks can grow inside the egg.

Even after the chicks hatch, the mother hen cares about keeping the chicks safe and warm. The chicks will cuddle close to the hen and she will keep them safe and warm with her wings. The chicks follow the hen and she guides them along their path.

Can you believe that Jesus once talked about chickens? In fact, there is a verse in the Bible that says, "I have desired to gather your children together as a hen gathers her brood under her wings. . . ."

That means God's love is much like the love a mother hen gives to her chicks. God cares about us and wants to keep us safe and warm just like a mother hen wants to keep her chicks safe and warm.

The Bible tells us to stay close to God for comfort and guidance. We want to follow God, because God loves and cares about us so much and that is a very special thing!

Let's pray—

Dear God, we know mother hens love their chicks very much. Thank you for giving us that same kind of love. Amen.

27
God's Wallet

Object A wallet with money, pictures, other special items

Scripture Luke 15:1-10

Theme God's Love Is Wonderful and Great

I BROUGHT MY WALLET WITH ME TODAY. What are some things found in a wallet. *(Wait for a response.)*

Sometimes we put special things in our wallets. Let me show you what I have in mine. *(Adapt this section for your wallet.)*

I have a little silver cross that a friend gave to me. This cross reminds me that God loves me. I have a Band-Aid tucked in this section—you never know when you might need a Band-Aid!

Here's my library card. And I have many pictures of my family in my wallet because I love and care for them. *(Take a minute and name some people in the pictures.)* I'm sure all of your parents have pictures of you in their wallets because they love and care for you.

I like to think that the best thing about God is his love for us. It never matters what we do or say. Even though God might not be pleased with our action, he never will take his love away from us.

God's love for us will last forever. There is nothing in this world that will take God's love away from each one of us. Nothing is stronger than God's love. In fact, God loves you so much that if God had a wallet, your picture would be in it.

Let's pray—

Dear God, thank you for the great and wonderful love you have for each of us. Thank you that nothing will ever take that love away. Amen.

28

Jesus Is the Bread of Life

Object A variety of symbols and a loaf of bread
Scripture Luke 24:13-35
Theme Bread for Our Souls

I used a variety of symbols from sports and our community. Choose symbols from your community (high school mascot, restaurant, etc.) that children will recognize.

I HAVE SEVERAL THINGS IN this bag. Let's look at them together.

What do you think of when you see this shirt? *(the Chicago Bulls.)*

What do you think of when you see this? *(McDonalds.)* When you see this? *(Bearcat paw.)*

Now what do you think of when you see a loaf of bread? *(Several answers will come. Lead the children in thinking of Jesus as the Bread of Life.)*

There is a story in the Bible which will soon be read that tells us that the disciples recognized Jesus when he broke bread with them.

One day the disciples were walking along the road and having a discussion with Jesus, although they weren't sure that it was Jesus. They invited Jesus to stay with them.

Breaking bread together was something that Jesus and the disciples did many times together. As soon as they saw Jesus break the bread, they knew it was Jesus.

We have also heard Jesus talked about as the Bread of Life. We all know that we need bread to eat so that our bodies are healthy. But, praying, following Jesus, learning about Jesus, and living our lives the way Jesus wants us to all keep our spiritual life healthy.

Both bread for our body and bread for our souls are important in our lives. Breaking bread is a symbol for the life and love of Jesus. The next time you hear of breaking the bread, think about Jesus.

After our prayer if any of you would like to pull a piece of bread off this loaf and take it with you to eat, you may.

Let's pray—

Dear God, thank you for the bread we eat to keep our bodies strong. Thank you, too, for the Bread of Life which strengthens our souls. Amen.

29

God's Signature

Object A Variety of Signatures
Scripture John 1:29-34
Theme God Gives His Signature in a Variety of Ways

*D*O YOU KNOW WHAT A SIGNATURE IS? It is the signing of your name. Most of you know how to write your name. Maybe you print it or write it in cursive.

Those of you who are in school know that you need to put your signature on all your schoolwork so the teacher knows whose work he or she is looking at. Our signature tells other people who we are.

Each person in my Sunday school class put their signature on this paper today. Do you see how they are all different?

Signatures reveal a little bit about us. Some people have messy signatures and maybe that says they are in a hurry. Some people have very small signatures. Maybe that says they like things neat and orderly. Other people sign their names with fancy writing.

Do you know that God has a signature? In fact, God has lots of signatures. We don't see the writing of his signature—G-o-d. But we see God's signatures all around us. God reveals his goodness all around us, and I like to think of those things as his signatures.

We see the beauty of nature—snow, trees, flowers, and many other things. All of the signs of nature are God's signatures.

We see God's signature in people who need our help and concern.

We see God's signature in the people around us that care for us and help us.

We see God's signature in the good feelings we get as we worship him.

There are many places to see God's signature. Open your eyes and ears. Look and listen to our beautiful world. Look at your family and friends.

And think about God and the blessings God has given us in many signatures!

Let's pray—

Dear God, your beautiful signatures are all around us. Thank you for your blessings, and remind us to look for your signature. Amen.

30

*M*ake Room for the New

Object   New pair of shoes

Scripture   John 3:1-17

Theme   Old Habits Or Things Must Leave for the New to Be Present

I used shoes for this activity. However, you could use a hat, gloves, or some other object that gives the illustration that we need to let go of old ways and let the new take place.

GOOD MORNING! LAST WEEK I bought a new pair of shoes. I really like these shoes, but I haven't worn them yet. My old sneakers needed to be replaced. I had worn them for a long time, and they even had a hole in them.

I like these shoes so much that I want to show you how they look when I have them on. Let's see. Hmm—I hope I didn't buy the wrong size.

Do you think my feet grew? What's wrong? I have to take my other shoe off. That's right. I can't put my new shoe on over my old shoe!

It is the same in our lives. We need to get rid of the old and put in the new. There are many times throughout our lives when we need to put away the old and add the new. You all quit crawling and started walking. Each year in school you leave one grade and move to another.

It is the same with our relationship with God. We can put away the old and become new when we believe and trust in God. When we tell God that we believe and trust in him, our lives become new. Our old habits and mistakes can be put behind us, and we try hard to live our lives so that we and our actions are pleasing to God.

All through our lives our relationship with God changes. We know God is always with us. As we grow and learn more about God, our relationship with God grows, too. Be willing to grow and learn new things!

Let's pray—

Dear God, thank you for making us new as we believe and trust in you. Please continue to guide us so that our actions will be pleasing to you. Amen.

31
Lots of Decisions

Object   A restaurant menu
Scripture   John 6:60-69
Theme   God Lets Us Make Our Own Decisions

DO YOU LIKE TO EAT AT A RESTAURANT? Eating at a restaurant is one of my favorite things to do.

What do you do when the server gives you the menu? You look at it, see what is available to order, and you make a decision on what you would like for your meal.

It might be a hard decision because there are so many items on the menu. Sometimes after you receive the food you order, you think another choice of food might have been better and you regret your decision.

It is important to make your decisions carefully. The food we choose to eat is important for our bodies, so we must decide on healthy food.

There are many decisions we need to make other than just what to eat. We decide on our friends, what activities we do, what we watch on TV, and many other things. What we decide to do affects our life, so it is important to make a responsible decision.

We are always going to need to make decisions.

God is giving us the opportunity to decide things for ourselves and to make choices.

We are fortunate to be able to make decisions. Many people in our world don't have a variety of food or clothes to choose from.

God has given us many blessings. One of the those blessings is being able to make decisions, so it is important to make decisions wisely. With God's help we can do that.

Let's pray—

Dear God, thank you for letting us make our own decisions. Guide us as we try to do so wisely. Amen.

32

We Are All Different and Special

Object Variety of autumn objects—hat, pumpkin, football, colored leaves

Scripture Romans 12:3-5

Theme We Are All Important in God's Plan

GOOD MORNING! I have a lot of things in this bag that are important clues to something I want you to guess.

Let's look at them. First, a hat. A hat keeps us warm. Next, a football. Lots of you like to play football, don't you? Next, a pumpkin. Last, colored leaves.

Any guesses? You're right! We have changed seasons from summer to autumn. All of those things let us know it is the season of autumn.

Let's look at these colored leaves together. *(Talk about each leaf—big or small, what color, etc.)* All of these leaves have added beauty to our world. First they were just tiny buds on the tree in springtime. Gradually, as the air got warmer, the leaves grew and turned green. Then they were beautiful as the trees were very full in the summer.

Now we are enjoying the change of color in the fall.

Each leaf was important on the tree. Without the leaves the trees could not have been as big and beautiful, so we know that each leaf is important. Each leaf had a very special place on a tree. Even if just some of the leaves were missing, the tree wouldn't have been as big and beautiful.

Each one of us is important in God's world, too. We don't all look the same. We don't all act the same. But each one of us is important to God just the way we are.

We all add beauty in our own way to God's special world. And we can help in God's world by being kind, helping others, and remembering to say thank you to God. We add beauty to this world when we are kind, thoughtful, and concerned for other people.

We can be thankful that God cares for each one of us and that God thinks each one of us is very special.

Let's pray—

Dear God, thank you that we each have a special place in your world. Guide us as we look for ways we can help each other. Amen.

33
*U*nique *Gifts*

Object Inkpad and paper
Scripture Romans 12:6-8
Theme Everyone Has Unique Gifts

NOT ONE OF US IS EXACTLY the same as another person. Each of us is made special by God.

Not only do we have different hair, different eyes, or are taller or shorter than other people, but our fingerprints are even different.

Watch as I make my fingerprint. *(Make a fingerprint and show it to the children.)* This fingerprint is unique. No one else in the entire world has a print exactly like it.

Each of us are born with special prints. We are also born with special talents.

When you are born, your parents don't know if you will play the piano well, or draw well, or be a good ball player. But God knows. God has given each of us special gifts and he has made each of us unique. It is our job to learn what our talents are and then practice to develop our talents.

God planned for each of us to be special. We are not exactly like anyone else. We shouldn't try to be like anyone else. God loves us exactly the way we are.

If you wish you could do something as well as someone else, or you wish you had the cool sneakers that someone else has, remember God made you special. And God loves you just the way you are.

Let's pray—
Dear God, thank you that we are very special to you. Help us to remember that specialness. Amen.

34

A Consecration Service

Object None

Scripture 1 Corinthians 12: 4-11

Theme Children Are an Important Part of the Church

I USUALLY BRING AN OBJECT to talk about. But today I am going to tell you about something which will happen a little later in the church service.

There will be a consecration service. *Consecrate* is a big word but it means to dedicate and promise.

The people who will participate in the consecration service are members of the church board, deacons, teachers, prayer disciples, and other volunteers. These people are offering their time and talents to do jobs in the church. The people in the congregation will offer their support to these people.

Not only are there jobs in the church for adults to do, but there are jobs for children to do, too.

Can you think of any jobs for children? You are doing a job by coming to Sunday school. You can put a coin in the offering plate. You are learning by coming for the story and by looking at the children's bulletin. Someday you will be big enough to be adult leaders in the church.

By doing the jobs we mentioned for children, you are learning things that will help you to be a good leader when you are an adult. Each of you have special talents that help you to be important helpers and leaders in our church even now.

Sometimes, people say that children are the church of the future. That's true, but each of you are also an important part of our church right now!

When the consecration service happens in a few minutes, think about the jobs you can do for the church as children.

Let's pray—

Dear God, help us to always be willing workers for you. Amen.

35

*F*amily *Teamwork*

Object An ant farm
Scripture 1 Corinthians 12:12-26
Theme Families Need to Work as Teams

I BROUGHT SOME CREATURES with me this morning. Let's look.

Look at this ant farm! All of these ants are creatures created by God. And all of these ants have special jobs to do. The ants work very hard in this farm.

Some ants are responsible for finding food. Sometimes they carry things much bigger and heavier than they are. Some ants dig new rooms. Some ants drag away trash. Some ants carry seeds. Others store food. This farm of ants works together as a team. They are a family that works together.

Each of our families needs to work together as a team, too. Each family is different. Some families have a mom, dad, and children. Some families are grandparents and children. Some families are either a mom or a dad, and children. Some families don't have children.

No matter who is in the family, or how the family is made up, each family member needs to work as a member of a team with special responsibilities.

We have families that we live with, but we are also

members of another important family. That family is the family of God. Our church family works together in this church to serve God.

Some of our church family members are musical. Some are teachers. Some of our church family members are planners and organizers. All of us are member's of God's family. We should work like a team in serving God.

It's great to be a member of a family and to work as a team. And, it is especially great to be a member of God's family with God's great love.

Let's pray—
Dear God, we are thankful for our families. And we are glad to be a member of your great family, too. Help us all work together in your love as a team. Amen.

36

God's Great Gift

Object   A baby or toddler
Scripture   Galatians 1:15
Theme   We All Have the Great Gift of Life

WE HAVE SOME VERY YOUNG CHILDREN here for the story today. Are you surprised to see babies with us?

Roxann *(or whomever you invited)* brought her new baby, Sarah, who is five weeks old. I brought Joel, who is fifteen months old. I asked Roxann to bring Sarah, and I brought Joel for a special reason. I want to talk about a great gift that God has given us.

Look at baby Sarah with her tiny fingers and toes. She smiles and cries and is fun to cuddle. Baby Sarah has God's great gift. Joel has God's great gift, too. He walks all over the place and explores and is learning about the world.

All of you have God's great gift. You can do so many things. You can play games, read, learn, and do special things for others.

All of the grown-ups have God's great gift, too. God's great gift that I am talking about is life. All of us have life. God has given each of us special talents and abilities for our lives.

It is up to us to develop those special talents that God has given us. There are many ways that God might use us. We need to let him guide our lives and trust him to lead us through our lives.

God's gift to us is life. What we do with our life is our gift back to God.

Let's pray—

Dear God, thank you for your gift of life. Guide our lives so that what we do is a gift to you. Amen.

37

We Are All Connected

Object A ball of yarn
Scripture Galatians 6:9-10
Theme We Are All Connected in God's Family

Children really enjoy this yarn activity! Be sure to explain the procedure before you begin. The explanation helps to keep this a calm, peaceful activity!

THIS MORNING WE ARE going to try something different for our story. You need to listen carefully.

I am going to hold on to this end of the yarn. Then I'm going to pass it to someone else. That person will hold on to the yarn and pass it to someone else. That person will do the same, and then the next person will do it until we are all connected.

You must remember to hold onto the yarn. Ready? Let's try it.

Okay! We are all holding on to the yarn. And we are all connected. We are all woven together by this yarn. If I wiggle my part of the yarn it causes a vibration throughout the rest of the yarn. If I pull it, you feel it.

In our families we are also connected and woven together. Just like the yarn bonds us together, there is a bond within each of our families. We care about one another. Sometimes we get mad at each other. Sometimes we cry together. And lots of times we laugh and have fun together.

Not only are each of us bound together with family members, but we are bound and woven together in a very special family—the family of God.

As members of this church family we worship God together, have fun together, laugh together, and sometimes, cry together.

It is special to be a member in a family. It is also special to be a member of the family of God. To be bound and woven together with God is a very special thing to be.

Let's pray—

Dear God, thank you for our families. Thank you, too, that we are bound and woven together with you in your family. Amen.

38
*K*eep a Tight Hold

Object Kite

Scripture Ephesians 4:29

Theme We Need to Control Our Actions Like a Kite
Is Controlled by a String

*H*AVE ANY OF YOU EVER SAILED A KITE? Isn't
it fun? It is also very beautiful!

When my family goes to the shore each summer,
we enjoy seeing people sail kites on the beach. The
kites are colorful and sail along very nicely in the
breeze from the ocean.

You have to have a nice breeze and an open area to
be able to sail a kite. You also need a string to be able to
control the kite.

What would happen if you tried to sail a kite without a string? You're right, it doesn't work. What would
happen if you tried to sail a kite and left go of the
string? It would fall down. If you only had hold of the
string by the very end, and a gust of wind grabbed the
kite, it could sail away from you.

That string is very important in the success of sail-
ing a kite. It controls the kite. The kite can get out of
control without the string and the big gust of wind.

Like a kite, our words and actions can get out of

control. Sometimes unkind words fly out of our mouths. Sometimes untrue words fly out of our mouths. Sometimes we are unkind to other people. Sometimes some people get really out of control and steal things or hurt other people.

We need to have strong control on our words and actions. Instead of unkind words, we need to let kind words come from our mouths. Instead of untrue words, we need to let true words come from our mouths. Instead of being unkind, we need to be kind to others. We need to keep good control and not steal and hurt other people.

Even though we try to have really good control on our words and actions, there are times when we slip and lose control. But, you know, God is always willing to forgive us when we admit we lost control and are sorry.

Let's pray—

Dear God, we try to keep control. Guide us and help us as we control our words and actions. Thank you for forgiving us when we do lose control. Amen.

39
Connected Hearts

Object Red construction paper, scissors

Scripture Philippians 1:3-11

Theme We Connect Our Hearts with Others as We Share with Them

Children love to see this transformation take place. For your calmness and comfort, practice enough ahead of time so that the folding/cutting occurs without hesitation.

WATCH AS I FOLD THIS piece of paper. *(Fold like an accordion.)* The paper is folded like an accordion. I can cut a corner off. And another corner.

Then I can cut a curve at the top corner. And I cut another curve on the other top corner. When the paper is unfolded, it has formed a string of connected hearts.

There are other ways that hearts can be connected. When we care for other people, we are sharing our hearts. We are showing them we care for and love them by what we do for them.

God wants us to care for and love others. What are some ways you can care for others? *(Wait for response and affirm the children as they respond with ways to love others.)*

All of those acts are ways you can show others you care. When you do those things, you are sharing and connecting your heart with others.

So, just as these paper hearts are connected, our hearts in this church can be connected as we love and care for others with our talents and resources. As we do that, we are sharing love from God's heart.

Let's pray—

Dear God, thank you that we have so much to share with others. Help us share our hearts with them. Amen.

40

I t's Good to Share

Object Bags of M & M's for each child
Scripture Philippians 2:3-4
Theme Unselfishness

I BROUGHT MY FAVORITE KIND of candy with me today—M & M's.

Ever since I have been little like you, M & M's have been my favorite. I like them because they are little, colorful, and chocolate. *(Mention a candy and tell a story that fits your life.)*

When I was growing up, we lived several miles from a store. So it was a special occasion when one of my parents would say we were going to town. We didn't go to a store as often as most of you go to Sheetz. *(Mention a convenience store in your area.)*

I always looked forward to a treat of M & M's on our shopping trip. When I got a bag of M & M's, I was not excited about sharing them with my brothers. And, sometimes I didn't.

But I knew I was being selfish. I always felt better when I shared the M & M's with my brothers.

I know all of you are sometimes faced with being selfish or unselfish. Maybe someone else would like a turn on the swing which you are using. Or maybe someone would like to look at a book you are using.

You are being kind and unselfish when you share. And the best part is, when you share you are showing God's love.

I brought something to share with you today. I have a bag of M & M's for each of you. I want you to enjoy some of them, but I also want you to share some of them with another person.

When you share these M & M's, you will be doing something unselfish. And being unselfish is a good thing to be.

Let's pray—

Dear God, sometimes we don't always feel like we want to share. But help us remember it is good to be unselfish. Amen.

41

Getting Along with Others

Object Small bags, each holding two Hershey's Kisses

Scripture Philippians 4:1-9

Theme Getting Along with Others Takes Work

GOOD MORNING! There are several things each of us has to do everyday. What do you think we need to do?

(Wait for responses. Adjust this paragraph accordingly with the responses. Guide the children to see that we need to get along with other people.)

First, we need to get up. We need to eat everyday. We need to brush our hair, and brush our teeth. Some of us need to go to work. Some of you need to go to school. We all need to play. And all of us need to get along with other people.

Sometimes getting along with people is easy. You may really like the person and have a lot of fun. But sometimes, getting along is very hard. No matter how much you like someone, there may be times when you don't get along very well. You may feel tired and grumpy and just don't feel like being nice to someone.

There may be times when someone isn't kind to you. That really hurts.

There are a lot of things we can do to help our friendships. We can be kind. We can share. Sometimes, a hug or a kiss is good. Sometimes we need to forgive. It is good to play and do things together, and sometimes, it is important to be alone for awhile.

All the time we need to know that God will help us with our friendships. We can always pray to God about our friendships and ask for God's guidance and help as we get along with other people.

I have something special for you after we say our prayer. It is a small bag with two Hershey's Kisses. One of the kisses I am giving to you because I like each of you, I care about you, and I like to get along with you.

Remember, there are two Hershey's Kisses in here. I want you to give the second one to someone you care about.

Let's pray—
Dear God, help us always to care for and love other people. Thank you for your great love to us. Amen.

42

*P*ut It in Your Pocket

Object Items that would be in your pocket
Scripture 1 Thessalonians 3:13
Theme Store God's Love in Your Pockets

DO ANY OF YOU HAVE A POCKET in the clothes you are wearing? Check and see—stand up if you need, too. *(Wait for a response.)*

Do you have anything in those pockets today? Maybe you are carrying a coin for the offering plate or hankies.

Pockets are great places for carrying things. Some people keep their wallets or keys in their pockets. Some children put all sorts of things such as rocks, crayons, and candy in their pockets.

It is really important to remember to take everything out of your pockets and be sure they are empty before you put them in the laundry basket.

Our mind, heart, and soul are a lot like pockets. We can empty the pockets of our mind, heart, and soul to God in prayer.

We can't give God the rocks, crayons, keys, or those kind of things that are in our pockets. But we can take all of our sad feelings and happy feelings and thoughts and share them with God through prayer.

We can empty our pockets to God, but we can also fill our pockets—our heart, and mind, and soul—with the great promises God gives us.

We can store God's promises and God's great love in the pockets of our soul.

Let's pray—

Dear God, thank you for caring about us. We are glad you care for us and listen to us. Let us fill our pockets with your great love. Amen.

43

T reasure from God

Object Small box covered in gold foil, treasures from God written on slips of paper

Scripture 2 Timothy 1:1-14

Theme God Has Given Us Many Treasures

IN THIS BOX ARE TREASURES from God. Each one take a turn and pick a piece of paper from the treasure box. See what is written on the paper *(love, peace, prayer, relationship with God, kindness, family)*.

Often when we think of treasures, we think of gold, silver, diamonds, and other jewels. Those jewels are valuable in a monetary sense, but God has given us other special treasures.

Those are the treasures we drew from the treasure chest. We can feel God's treasures in the love of family and friends. We can see God's treasures in our world around us. We can feel God's treasures inside of ourselves. We know that God is with us all the time, and that is a very special treasure.

Sometimes we get so busy and hurried in our lives that we forget to think about and remember our special treasures from God. But our treasures from God are special and are important in our lives every minute of every day.

Keep your eyes open. Watch for God's treasures all around. As you feel happiness and love from your family and friends, remember those things are part of God's treasures.

Talking to God in prayer is also a wonderful treasure. Use that treasure often! In fact, let's use it right now!

Let's pray—

Dear God, you have given each of us so many treasures. Thank you for the treasures and help us to keep the treasures first in our lives. Amen.

44

*W*e Can Feel Satisfied

Object   A picture of or an actual cornucopia
Scripture   Joel 2:21-27
Theme   Feel Satisfaction

S OME PEOPLE CALL THIS A HORN of plenty. This gathering of harvest vegetables reminds us to be thankful for and satisfied with all God has given us.

Let's look together at what is in it. Just say out loud what you see. *(Take a minute to name what is in the horn of plenty.)*

In the first book of the Bible, which is Genesis, we read the story about God creating the heavens and the earth. In that story, we hear of all God created—the sun, moon, stars, earth, water, land, animals, people.

After these creations we hear phrases like, "And God saw it was good." That sounds to me as though God stood back, rested, and felt satisfaction at all the projects he had accomplished.

We can feel satisfaction at what we accomplish, too. It is okay even for children to pause for a few minutes and think about what you have just completed. Maybe it is a test at school, or homework, or a job your parents assign to you.

We can also feel satisfaction at what we have in life.

All of us are blessed with family and friends and plenty of clothing and food to eat. The horn of plenty reminds us that we have many things to feel thankful for and satisfied about.

This Thursday is Thanksgiving Day. This special day is a good day to think of all the blessings God has given us.

Sometimes we want more—more toys, or clothes, or money. But God gives us what we need. We can show our satisfaction for our blessings by being thankful, not only on Thanksgiving Day, but every day of the year.

Let's pray—

Dear God, help us always to find satisfaction at what we do and what we have. Amen.

45

A Restful Time

Object Music flash cards with symbols of musical rests

Scripture Hebrews 4:9-13

Theme Rest Is Good for Us

I BROUGHT SOME CARDS that have symbols on them. Do any of you know what these symbols mean?

They are musical rests. This is a quarter rest. This is a half rest. And this is a whole rest. A whole rest means that the musician needs to be silent during a measure where a whole rest is printed.

Some people might say that a whole rest means it is a measure of nothing. But it is a measure of something. The composer, the person who wrote the music, wrote the silent measure for a very special reason. He or she planned for the silent measure, which fits carefully onto the entire piece of music.

These symbols indicate rest in music. But people need rest, too. Do your mothers ever tell you it is time to be still and rest?

Sometimes children are so busy playing that they don't think they have time to rest. But, rest for us, just like a musical rest, is not a time of nothing.

God planned rest for us. The Bible says we should rest on the Sabbath. That is a full measure of rest for us. We need to put aside our work and use that measure of rest to be thankful, think about our life, and get energized again.

Let's pray—

Dear God, we are all busy with activities in our lives, even children, but teach us to be still and rest. Amen.

46

*D*on't Wear a Mask

Object   A variety of masks

Scripture   James 5:13-16

Theme   We Don't Need to Mask Our Feelings When
We Pray

I BROUGHT SOMETHING WITH ME this morning.
Let's see what it is. I have a black mask, a pumpkin
mask, and a Big Bird mask.

At Halloween or at parties some people wear
masks, or paint their faces, to pretend they are someone they really aren't. They are trying to hide their
identity from other people.

Other times, though we don't have masks on, we
don't let others know our true feelings. That is like
wearing a mask. We might not tell people how we tru-
ly feel. We might keep a lot of feelings covered inside.

But, we never should wear a mask on our feelings
when we talk to God in prayer because God knows
each of us very well. God wants to know when we are
feeling sad, or angry, or happy.

You don't always have to pray aloud. You can pray
silently so only God hears. You can pray sitting, or
standing, or kneeling, or with your hands folded or unfolded.

I once heard that God looks at our heart condition, not our body position when we pray. You can pray at bedtime or mealtime, or church, or at school, or any time you need to talk to God.

You can pray not only for yourself, but for other people, too. God listens and cares about everything you say in your prayers.

As you develop your relationship with God through prayer, don't wear a mask on your feelings.

Let's pray—

Dear God, we thank you for the privilege of being able to tell you everything in prayer. We know that you care about all of us. Amen.

47
*W*ho *Cares?*

Object   Picture of bike riding
Scripture   1 Peter 5:7
Theme   God Cares for Us

*H*OW MANY OF YOU KNOW HOW to ride a bike which does not have training wheels?

Riding a bike is much fun, but learning how to do it well requires patience and practice. First you need to learn how to stay balanced when you are on the bike.

Then, when you have just learned how to stay balanced, you must learn how to ride smoothly and how to turn corners easily.

Learning how to ride a bike is a special thing, but it is not easy. Everyone who has learned to ride a bike has had plenty of skinned elbows and knees. We can say sometimes we suffer when we learn how to ride a bike.

It hurts when we suffer, but we know that God suffers with us. There is a verse in the Bible which says, "Cast all your anxiety on him, because he cares for you." He even cares when you fall off your bike.

We receive much care from God. God has given us a wonderful world to enjoy. God provides food, sunshine, and rain. God has given us parents who love and protect us. God comforts us and helps us with our problems. God constantly watches over us.

We know we will still have problems to deal with. But we also know God will go through those problems right along with us.

Let's pray—

Dear God, thank you for the loving care you give us. Help us to remember that your loving arms will always be there for us for comfort and guidance. Amen.

48

Names for Jesus

Object A baby name book

Scripture Luke 21:25-32

Theme There Are Many Descriptive Names for Jesus

THIS BOOK IS TITLED, *The Best Baby Name Book in the Whole World.* Many parents look in a book like this to search for names for a baby.

This book tells where the name is from and what it means. I looked up the names of the children who usually come for the story to see what your names mean. Let me tell you what I found.

(I prepared a list ahead of time of the names of the children who generally come for the story. I listed the names in alphabetical order in an effort at time management. There were some visitors, so I took a minute to look for the meaning of their names.)

Your name identifies who you are. And sometimes people are given nicknames by family and friends that describe the person.

When Jesus was born, Mary and Joseph did not have a baby name book like this to use in search of a name. Instead, an angel told Joseph during a dream that the baby's names should be Jesus, which means "savior."

The name Jesus described him as Savior of the world. There are many descriptive names for Jesus. Some are Yahweh, Our Father, Morning Star, Emmanuel, and Prince of Peace.

Today is the beginning of Advent, which is a time of preparation and waiting for the birthday of Jesus. Advent is a really good time to think about the greatness of Jesus and what his being the Savior of the World means for us.

Let's pray—

Dear Jesus, thank you for the specialness of you and all that you mean to the world. Amen.

49

A Special Request

Object   No object, but a robe with a hood is needed
Scripture   Luke 1:26-38
Theme   God Asks Ordinary People to Do Special
Tasks

(I began the story by explaining that I was going to tell Mary's part of the Christmas story. At the beginning of the story I put the hood of the robe on my head. I concluded the story by removing the hood and giving a summary.)

TODAY I AM GOING TO TELL the story as a different character *(put on the hood).* My name is Mary. I know some of you know about me from the Christmas story.

Can you tell what I did *(wait for response)*? I was the mother of Jesus. I would like to tell you a little of how that all came to be.

When I was about thirteen an angel of the Lord named Gabriel came to visit me. Gabriel told me that I would give birth to a son who would be named Jesus. He would be called the Son of the Most High.

I told the angel that this could just not be. Why me? I was just a common, ordinary girl. Gabriel told me that I had found favor with God.

Well, I believed and trusted God. I wanted to do my best to obey God and so I said, "Let it be," which meant I was willing to do this special task.

At that time I was engaged to a man named Joseph. This meant we were to be married. When Joseph learned I was to have a child, he wasn't sure he wanted to marry me. But an angel appeared to Joseph and told him it was okay to marry me.

We needed to go to Bethlehem to pay our taxes. It was a long trip! Can you imagine—the trip took us about five days, because we walked and rode a donkey. Five days of travel is like a week of school for you!

When we arrived, Bethlehem was crowded and there was no room to rest. Finally an innkeeper let us stay in a stable and Jesus was born there.

It was a special night. There were animals in the stable. Soon shepherds arrived because they had seen a great star. The shepherds were the first outside the stable to know about the birth. Later kings arrived to worship Jesus and give him presents.

(Remove hood.) I told you the story in the character of Mary. God asked her to do a wonderful task by becoming the mother of Jesus.

In all our lives, at some point, there will be special things that we can do for God. Some will be easy. Some tasks will be hard. Some tasks you may not be sure you want to do.

You need to listen to what God would like you to do. Then, hopefully, your response will be like Mary's. Be willing and simply say, "Let it be."

As you go back to your seats, go with listening ears and willing hearts to be good servants of God.

50
The Star Was a Sign

Object Star ornaments from a Christmas tree
Scripture Isaiah 7:10-16
Theme The Star Guided People to Jesus

*D*O YOU KNOW WHAT SPECIAL DAY is coming this week? Christmas! I knew you would know!

All during our Advent season we have been waiting for the birthday of Jesus, which we celebrate on Christmas Day.

During the Christmas season we see all kinds of signs and symbols. We see trees, lights, presents, nativity scenes, candles, and stars.

The star is a very special sign of Christmas. Many people put a star on top of their Christmas tree and hang star ornaments on the tree.

I brought some star ornaments from our Christmas tree. I have a punched tin star and a bright yellow paper star.

Perhaps the star is one of the most important signs of Christmas because it was a special sign to others to travel to where Jesus was born.

We know that many people knew the star was a sign telling them that a king had been born. The Bible tells us the star provided a great light so that others could find Jesus. The star was a welcome and wonderful sign to them.

Everybody looks for signs. There are signs along the road as we travel. There are signs on TV. There are signs in the newspapers. All of these signs tell us to look better, feel better, and be better.

There is a great way for us to be better and that is to worship and follow Jesus Christ. When Jesus is present in our lives, we can be like a star which shines because his light is in us. His presence in our lives also provides us with a light that guides us, just as the shepherds followed the guiding light to the manger many years ago.

When you follow Jesus and try to live the way he wants us to live, you can be an example or a sign to others that following Jesus is good.

Let's pray—

Dear God, help us to follow you and be a shining star for you. Amen.

51

A Birthday Party

Object Pieces of cake
Scripture Luke 2:1-7
Theme Have a Birthday Party for Jesus

Before the children gathered, I cut small pieces of angel food cake so that each child could have one.

DO ANY OF YOU LIKE to go to a birthday party? Ah, I knew it! Lots of you do!

Birthday parties are a lot of fun! There are games, food, fun, and presents for the birthday person.

Are all of you excited and happy when it's your birthday? *(Expect a joyous response!)* I suspected that, too! Birthdays are special when we are helping someone else celebrate. Or when we ourselves are having a birthday.

Christmas is a very special birthday celebration. Whose birthday is it? Jesus'! We remember that Jesus was born in a building like a barn. And we remember that many, many people traveled to worship the baby Jesus and give him gifts. A lot of people were very happy that Jesus was born. They wanted to celebrate.

Sometimes, Christmas is so busy with other activities and projects that we forget we should be celebrating a special birthday. Sometimes we get so excited looking forward to special things that will be happening, and getting gifts, that it is easy to forget we should be celebrating the birth of Jesus.

Let's take a minute right now and help to celebrate this special birthday by singing "Happy Birthday" to Jesus. Everybody ready? Let's sing.

One special thing about birthday celebrations is having a piece of cake. So after our prayer, each one of you can get a piece of cake out of this basket. As you eat it, remember we are celebrating a very special birthday—the birthday of Jesus!

Let's pray—

Dear God, even though we get busy and excited this time of year, help us to remember this very special birthday. We thank you for the gift of Jesus. Amen.

52

*A*fter Christmas

Object   Heart stickers

Scripture   1 John 4:7-8

Theme   Keep the Love of Christmas in Your Heart
All Year

*D*ID EVERYONE HAVE A NICE CHRISTMAS?
Christmas is exciting and much fun, but is always a little sad to put away the Christmas items and take down the tree, isn't it?

This week at our house, we will be packing away the bows and ribbons, wrapping paper, tree ornaments, nativity scene, and most everything else that we used to decorate for Christmas. You will probably be doing the same thing at your house.

There is one thing about Christmas that we don't have to pack away. That is the love we felt at Christmas. At Christmas we do kind things for one another and that is a way to show love. We see love in people's faces as they sing Christmas music and do other special Christmas things. We don't have to pack that away until next year. We can try to keep that love in our hearts all year. Love is what Christmas is all about. Love is what Jesus is all about. We can keep that love with us always.

We can pack away all the reminders of Christmas, but we can keep the love of Christmas in our hearts all year long.

I'm giving each of you a heart sticker. You can put this sticker on your shirt now, or you can take it home with you and put it on something as long as you have your parents permission. Let this sticker remind you to keep the love of Christmas in your heart all year long.

Let's pray—

Dear God, help us keep the love of Christmas in our hearts all year long. Amen.

The Author

Donna McKee Rhodes, a licensed minister in the Church of the Brethren, is presently serving as Minister of Nurture at the Stone Church of the Brethren, Huntingdon, Pa. She attended Messiah College and has a B.S. in Early Childhood and Elementary Education from Juniata College.

Donna serves on Christian education committees at the district level of the Church of the Brethren. She has helped to lead a variety of teacher enrichment workshops.

She has always lived in central Pennsylvania and grew up on a dairy farm near McVeytown. She presently lives in Huntingdon with her husband, Loren, a professor of computer science at Juniata College, and their children Erica (1984), Aaron (1986), and Joel (1991).

Donna enjoys a variety of crafts and playing the piano.